THE OFFICIAL
Liverpool FC
ANNUAL 2012

Written by Paul Eaton

Designed by Cavan Convery

A Grange Publication

© 2011. Published by Grange Communications Ltd., Edinburgh under licence from The Liverpool Football Club and Athletic Grounds Ltd.

Printed in the EU.

ISBN: 978-1-908221-28-5

£7.99

Contents

New owners, new manager, new players – it's a new era for Liverpool Football Club and in the official 2012 annual we bring you closer than ever to your Kop idols.

2010-11 was a season of change both on and off the pitch at Anfield as the Reds fell under new ownership, Kenny Dalglish made an emotional return and millions were spent in the transfer market to bolster the squad, with Andy Carroll and Luis Suarez arriving to form a new-look deadly front-line duo.

With optimism high that success could be just around the corner for the rejuvenated Reds, we go behind the scenes at Anfield with exclusive interviews with the manager and key players, all of whom will be looking to play their part in bringing a new era of success to Liverpool FC.

There are also quizzes, posters and other special exclusive features to keep you entertained in the only Official Liverpool FC Annual.

SEASON REVIEW
2010/11

August

Roy Hodgson's Liverpool reign kicked off with a home game against Arsenal, and the Reds appeared set for three points after leading through David Ngog's second half goal. But Anfield hearts were broken in stoppage time when Pepe Reina uncharacteristically spilled a ball into his own net to gift the Gunners a point.

In the Europa League Hodgson guided his men to an opening group game victory over Trabzonspor, but in the league we went down to our first defeat in our first away game as Manchester City cruised to a 3–0 success at Eastlands.

A 2–1 victory in the return clash at Trabzonspor ensured smooth progress into the group stages of European competition, while a solitary Fernando Torres strike was enough to give Hodgson his first league victory as Liverpool boss against West Brom.

September

A dull goalless draw at Birmingham followed before we continued our impressive European form with a 4–1 demolition of Steaua Bucharest at Anfield.

The month was to take a turn for the worse after that, however, as a defeat at arch-rivals Manchester United was followed by a Carling Cup exit at the hands of Northampton at Anfield. The Cobblers ran out winners via a penalty shoot-out to leave the home supporters looking on disbelievingly.

October

October was a month which will be remembered more for events off the field than on it as, following a series of court cases, ownership of the Club was finally transferred to New England Sports Ventures (later renamed as Fenway Sports Group) under the leadership of John Henry and Tom Werner.

Sadly, the positive news of finally having new owners didn't materialise into positive results on the field as the Reds went down to a home defeat to Blackpool and then a derby defeat at Goodison – leaving the Club in the wrong half of the league table.

A home victory over Blackburn and a first away success of the season at Bolton halted the slide down the table.

Unfortunately, an immediate response to that disappointing Cup exit wasn't forthcoming as Sunderland left Anfield with a point and we laboured to a goalless European draw in Utrecht.

November

An inspired Steven Gerrard hat-trick rescued the Reds against Napoli at Anfield after the Italians had taken the lead, before Fernando Torres found his shooting boots to sink Chelsea in the league just a few days later.

A mixture of results followed over the rest of the month as the Reds struggled to find any consistency, with a draw at Wigan followed by a defeat at Stoke and then a convincing victory over West Ham before Tottenham netted a stoppage time winner to record a 2–1 win at White Hart Lane.

Unusually, Liverpool were still in the wrong half of the table with pressure growing from the supporters for results to start improving quickly.

December

December promised to be a better month for the Reds, but did not end as expected.

A 1–1 draw in Steaua Bucharest earned the Reds qualification into the knock-out stages of the Europa League before quick-fire goals from David Ngog, Ryan Babel and Maxi Rodriguez swept Aston Villa away at Anfield with arguably our most convincing display of the season so far.

But again consistency was the problem and Newcastle – with Andy Carroll in their ranks and on the scoresheet – running out 3–1 victors at St James Park. But there was worse to come in our final match of 2010 as relegation-battling Wolves left Anfield with all three points to heap more pressure on manager Roy Hodgson.

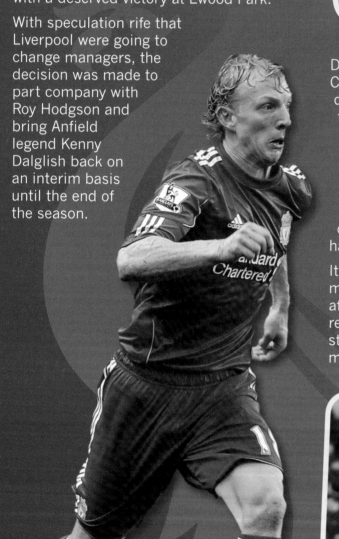

January

A late Joe Cole goal was the perfect way to see in the New Year as the Reds secured three points against Bolton at Anfield, but just a few days later Blackburn avenged their Anfield defeat earlier in the campaign with a deserved victory at Ewood Park.

With speculation rife that Liverpool were going to change managers, the decision was made to part company with Roy Hodgson and bring Anfield legend Kenny Dalglish back on an interim basis until the end of the season.

Dalglish's first assignment was an FA Cup third round trip to Old Trafford but, despite being cheered on by 9,000 travelling Kopites, an early United penalty proved to be the difference between the two sides.

Defeat at Blackpool and a derby draw with Everton followed before the Dalglish era found its winning touch with a convincing victory at Wolves and then a hard-fought home success over Fulham.

It was a milestone month in the transfer market as Liverpool sold Fernando Torres after the Spaniard handed in a transfer request and replaced him with Uruguay striker Luis Suarez and Newcastle front man Andy Carroll.

February

King Kenny's return had completely changed the mood inside the club – and the style of football on the field.

A 2–0 victory over Stoke – which included Suarez's first goal for the Reds · was followed by the highlight of the campaign so far as a Raul Meireles goal was enough to beat Chelsea at Stamford Bridge. Lingering thoughts of a relegation battle were suddenly turning into talk of a push for Europe.

A 1–0 aggregate success over Sparta Prague over two legs was enough to keep our European dreams alive before West Ham temporarily burst the bubble as they ran out 3–1 winners at Upton Park.

April

Andy Carroll got off the mark for the first time in a Liverpool shirt with a thumping drive as Liverpool defeated Manchester City at Anfield.

The following weekend another priceless point in the race for the top five was collected thanks to a 102nd minute

March

Manchester United were next up at Anfield and soon felt the full force of Suarez's brilliance, as the little Uruguayan tore Alex Ferguson's side apart to ensure the Kop had themselves a new hero. Dirk Kuyt was the matchwinner with a hat-trick of goals, but it was the performance of Suarez on the day which left Anfield purring.

Sadly the European dream ended at the hands of Portuguese outfit Braga, who progressed on the back of a 1-0 home leg victory before holding the Reds to a goalless stalemate at Anfield.

penalty from Dirk Kuyt at Arsenal. Having themselves taken the lead from the spot in stoppage time, the Gunners looked to be on their way to the victory they needed to keep their title hopes alive, but the Reds were not to be defeated and grabbed the

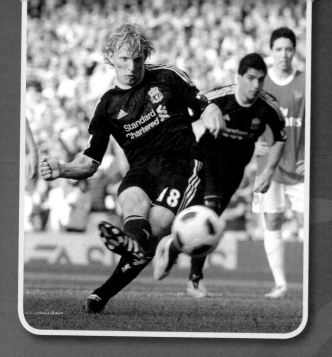

May

The defining month of May ultimately failed to go to plan for Liverpool. After another five goal display to see off Fulham at Craven Cottage and another convincing Anfield success to beat Newcastle, it went down to the final two games to see if fifth place could be reached.

Victory over Tottenham at Anfield would clinch a Europa League spot – but Spurs had other ideas and ran out 2–0 winners to ensure their destiny was in their hands on the final day of the campaign.

Ultimately it mattered little what result Tottenham earned as Liverpool failed to apply pressure with a victory at Aston Villa and instead went down to a 1–0 defeat to finish the season in sixth place.

most unlikely of points at the Emirates.

The confidence generated from that result then inspired Kenny's men to romp to a five goal victory over Birmingham at Anfield as thoughts of the top five – and European qualification for the following season – appeared to be looking more realistic.

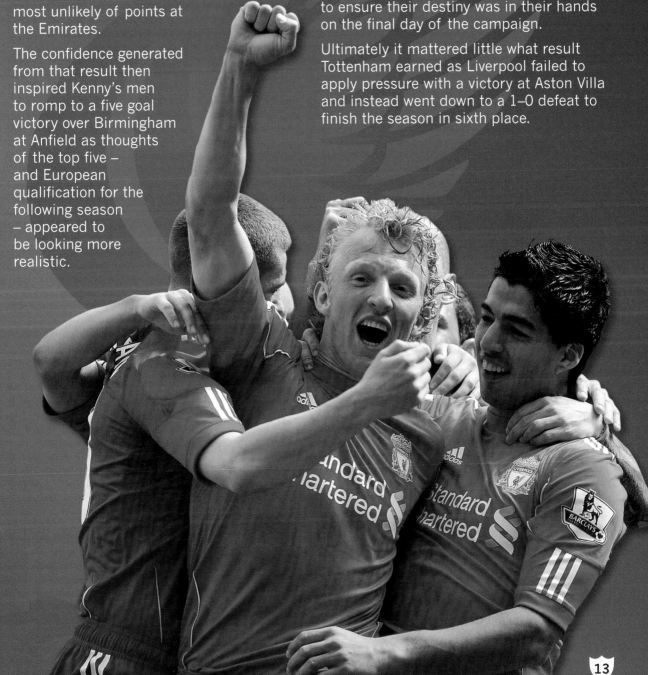

NEW SIGNING

Jordan Henderson

What was your initial reaction when you heard of Liverpool's interest?

I was flattered to know Liverpool were interested in me and, once I knew, it was a massive decision for me to make but also a massive opportunity.

How difficult was it for you to leave your local club?

Obviously it's hard to leave your local club. I'm a Sunderland lad, I've supported them all my life. But I'm really looking forward to the future now and obviously this is a massive opportunity for me. I'm really excited by it.

Did you seek advice from anyone about the decision?

Yes, obviously my family are all Sunderland fans as well, and it's pretty tough because I've had some great years there. I've been there since I was seven and I'll definitely miss it but, like I say, I'm looking forward to playing for Liverpool now.

There is a lot of competition for places here – is that something you're ready for?

Definitely. Coming to a massive club like Liverpool, there is always going to be competition. Hopefully I can keep working hard, keep improving, and get my chance on the pitch.

One player you'll be playing alongside is Steven Gerrard – how exciting is that for you and how big a role model has he been over the years?

He is one of the best players in the world, you want to be playing with him and training with him to try and improve yourself as a player. I've trained with him once (for England) and he was unbelievable, to be honest. I'm looking forward to it, and there are other good players here who can help me as well. Steven has been a massive, massive player for Liverpool for years now and he still is. Hopefully I can learn a lot from him.

And how does the thought of playing at Anfield every week sound?

I cannot wait to play at Anfield in front of the Liverpool fans and everything. I'm just excited and I want to get going.

Steven Gerrard on Jordan

"It's a really positive signing. Let's hope he is the next Steven Gerrard. That's what good football clubs do – they replace their best players. Liverpool needs a new Steven Gerrard and it will need a new Jamie Carragher.

"I saw Jordan at first hand for two or three days with England and he is a good player with energy."

What about Kenny Dalglish – are you looking forward to working with him over the next few years?

Yes, of course. He's done brilliantly since he came back to the club. He's done such a good job in such a short space of time. Hopefully he'll carry on doing that. I've already spoken to him and he's been brilliant with me so far. I'm really looking forward to it.

What kind of things were said between you?

I basically just thanked him for bringing me here. He seemed just as pleased as I was and that's obviously a good thing! It was all positive.

It's the start of an exciting new era at the club. What do you believe you can achieve here?

There is a lot to achieve. It's a massive club and we've seen over the last few months how good they are. So I'm just coming here to learn and try to improve my game and I'm sure that along the way there will be a lot of happy memories.

It must be in your mind that you could win trophies here?

Yes, of course. You come to a big club and you want to win things. Liverpool have won a lot in the past and hopefully there is a lot more to come in the future.

" Kenny Dalglish on Jordan

"It is fantastic for the football club to be able to attract hugely talented young footballers that have huge potential. Jordan is very mature for his age.

"He is respectful and his principles and everything else on and off the pitch are exemplary.

"Not only is he a talented footballer, he's a really good person as well. He loves his football and he is very appreciative of what Sunderland have done for him.

"You know of young players before of course but we were watching him since he came into the Sunderland first team and have been tracking him.

"We just need to go out and bring people to the football club that will raise the profile and standard of the performances that we have had - and I think Jordan falls into that category. People might turn around and say, 'Well you have people in there who have done really well'.

"Of course they have done well – and hopefully next year people will be saying the same thing about Jordan."

Lots of other clubs were reportedly interested in you – do you believe Liverpool is the best place for your development and for you to realise your football dreams?

Yes, definitely. Liverpool's definitely the place to help me come on as a player, and improve me. The club's going in the right direction and it can go as high as it wants.

You were the first major summer signing at Anfield – what's your message to the fans?

I'd like to tell them that I'm over the moon to be here and they will see me giving everything I've got in every game I play. Hopefully they'll enjoy watching me as much as I'll enjoy playing for this club.

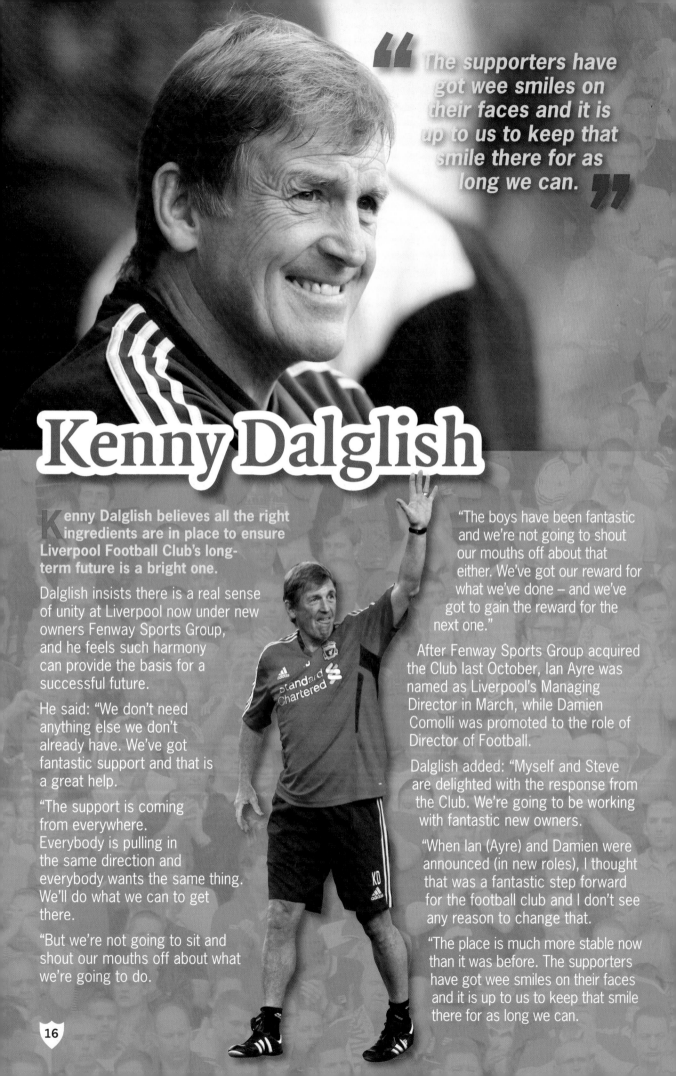

> **The supporters have got wee smiles on their faces and it is up to us to keep that smile there for as long we can.**

Kenny Dalglish

Kenny Dalglish believes all the right ingredients are in place to ensure Liverpool Football Club's long-term future is a bright one.

Dalglish insists there is a real sense of unity at Liverpool now under new owners Fenway Sports Group, and he feels such harmony can provide the basis for a successful future.

He said: "We don't need anything else we don't already have. We've got fantastic support and that is a great help.

"The support is coming from everywhere. Everybody is pulling in the same direction and everybody wants the same thing. We'll do what we can to get there.

"But we're not going to sit and shout our mouths off about what we're going to do.

"The boys have been fantastic and we're not going to shout our mouths off about that either. We've got our reward for what we've done – and we've got to gain the reward for the next one."

After Fenway Sports Group acquired the Club last October, Ian Ayre was named as Liverpool's Managing Director in March, while Damien Comolli was promoted to the role of Director of Football.

Dalglish added: "Myself and Steve are delighted with the response from the Club. We're going to be working with fantastic new owners.

"When Ian (Ayre) and Damien were announced (in new roles), I thought that was a fantastic step forward for the football club and I don't see any reason to change that.

"The place is much more stable now than it was before. The supporters have got wee smiles on their faces and it is up to us to keep that smile there for as long as we can.

"We've been happy with everything since we came in – the way the players have gone about their work, their attitude and commitment to training and taking it forward onto the pitch, and their desire to be successful.

"So everything was pointing in the right direction."

Dalglish's work in the transfer market over the summer saw a number of new players arrive at Anfield as Jordan Henderson, Charlie Adam, Stewart Downing, Alexander Doni and Jose Enrique all penned deals with the Reds.

"If they go about their work as well as they did at their previous clubs, then that will do us just fine.

"They want to win games at Liverpool just as at their previous clubs, so that's not a bad start. If they are level headed – which they are – and they are prepared to work hard – which they do – then we'll have a chance.

"We are pleased to have people here that appreciate what the football club is all about.

"Charlie was in Asia and saw what it was all about, and the other lads came to Norway and got an idea if they didn't already know.

"So they know what they are coming into and we are delighted to have them.

"The most important thing for us was getting people in and we've brought good people in.

"We've acted responsibly in the transfer market and we've also acted responsibly and respectfully with the owners, who have been fantastically supportive financially during the window.

"If there is a better owner that is as supportive as John Henry, then they have done very well for themselves because he's fantastically supportive."

Martin Kelly

Martin Kelly's breakthrough season at Anfield may have been cut short by injury – but Jamie Carragher believes the young defender has what it takes to be a regular at Anfield for years to come.

Kelly was keeping England international Glen Johnson out of the side with a series of commanding displays at right-back, before a hamstring injury at West Ham in February spelt the end of his campaign.

But with a new season having kicked off and Kelly back to full fitness, Carragher is expecting his Anfield teammate to continue to blossom – especially under the management of Kenny Dalglish.

"Since Kenny's come in, he's really taken off," said Carragher.

"I remember in his full debut against Lyon he was outstanding. Then he got injured and when that happens, it's difficult to get another chance.

"Since the United game, England's first-choice right-back (Glen Johnson) has been getting picked at left-back so that shows you how well he's done and how highly he's regarded.

"He's still young and his understanding of the game will develop with experience but he's already a fantastic athlete. I was in the stand against Everton and when he made that run past Leighton Baines, I thought it was Thierry Henry against me all those years ago. It was turbo charged.

"Modern full-backs need to be tall and Martin is very good at defending headers at the back post. His pace means he can get out of trouble when he does make a mistake. That ability to recover with speed was something I never had and he has that in abundance."

Kelly's chance last season came before the FA Cup tie at Manchester United when Glen Johnson was forced to pull out when his partner went into labour.

It was a stroke of luck for the England youth international – and an opportunity he grasped with both hands.

"I had a little bit of luck there and I've got the baby to thank for that I think!" Kelly said.

"It was good to play in a big game like that at Old Trafford. I remember missing the FA Youth Cup final there through injury and I was devastated, so it was good to go back and play there.

> **It has been good for me to play under Kenny and we have all got a massive lift with him coming back as manager.**

"Glen has been a good help for me. Just watching him on the pitch and seeing how good he is on the training ground has also helped me.

"He's a great lad and we get on well.

"I am enjoying playing at right-back but if the time comes when I'm needed to play centre back I will play there as well.

"It's good to be able to play anywhere in the back four if need be.

"Playing against Manchester United and then Everton are two of the biggest games I've ever been involved in."

He added: "It has been good for me to play under Kenny and we have all got a massive lift with him coming back as manager.

"Everyone wants to impress him and it shows on the training ground and it will soon start showing with results as well.

"The training is a lot more competitive now and that's a good thing for us.

"There's always strong competition at Liverpool and as long as you keep your standards as high as you can then you are going to stay in the team."

Spot the Ball

Can you spot which ball is in the correct place in the pictures below?

1

2

answers on pages 60-61

David Ngog

Stewart Downing

Stewart Downing spoke of his elation at completing his transfer to Liverpool and insisted the Reds were the only club he was interested in signing for.

The England international put pen to paper on a long-term deal with the club after tying up his switch from Aston Villa.

Now Downing can't wait to get his Liverpool career up and running and has set his sights on helping bring silverware back to Anfield.

"It's a great feeling and I'm very happy to be here," he said "It's been a long time coming and I've had to wait a few weeks, but I'm really pleased to be here.

"With the tradition, the manager and the players they have here, there was a big temptation to come here and once I knew of their interest, there was only one place I wanted to go."

He added: "It will be a great feeling to run out at Anfield. It's always nice to come and play here. The atmosphere is always great and the fans are brilliant.

"When I wanted to come to Liverpool, it was the first thing I thought of – playing at Anfield in front of those great fans. I'm really looking forward to it."

Downing became Liverpool's fourth major signing of a busy summer, following in the footsteps of Jordan Henderson, Charlie Adam and Alexander Doni.

And the winger is determined to repay Kenny Dalglish's faith in bringing him to Merseyside.

Downing said: "It would be nice to win something. I'm sure that's the same objective for everyone, not just me personally.

"My aim is to be in the team, to play well and give something back because the manager has pushed the boat out to get me here, so hopefully I can give him something back.

"Getting a few goals and a few assists for the lads up front, that's what I'm hoping for."

10 Facts about Stewart Downing

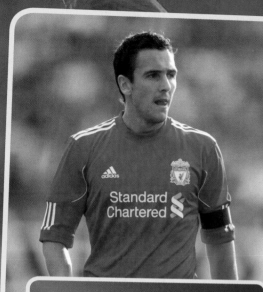

Downing has been involved in several charitable and community projects outside his playing career. He supports the nationwide 'No Messin' campaign along with freestyler Colin Nell and boxer Amir Khan, warning youngsters against playing on the railway lines.

He held a charity dinner with special guest boxer Ricky Hatton to raise funds for the Royal Victoria Infirmary in Newcastle-Upon-Tyne in February 2008. The hospital had cared for Vicky, Stewart's sister, who died of leukemia in 1993 at the age of four.

He joined Middlesbrough as a schoolboy and made his first-team debut for the club on April 24, 2002 in a Premier League match at Ipswich Town.

Stewart Downing was born in Middlesbrough on July 22, 1984.

After nine appearances for 'Boro, Downing was sent out on loan to fellow North-East club Sunderland in 2003, where he scored an impressive three goals in seven appearances. When he returned to Middlesbrough, he broke into the first team, going on to make a total of 206 appearances (scoring 22 goals) before leaving to join Aston Villa in the summer of 2009.

During his spare time, the wide man likes to DJ – demonstrating his skills in Ibiza among other places.

His Villa career spanned two years, during which time he tallied 75 appearances and scored eight goals.

His last appearance for the club was against Liverpool on the final day of 2010-11, a game in which he scored the only goal to help Villa to a 1-0 win.

Downing notched a total of nine Premier League assists for Aston Villa last season, more than any Liverpool player. He was joint ninth in the assists tally with Charlie Adam, Joey Barton, Peter Crouch, Peter Odemwingie, David Silva and Rafael Van der Vaart.

The 26-year-old made his England debut on March 9, 2005 in a friendly v Holland at Villa Park, coming on as a second-half substitute for Shaun Wright-Phillips. He currently has 27 caps for England.

When he was a kid, Downing's dad used to take him to training on his bike.

finishing in the top four is tougher than ever now

Jamie Carragher

Jamie Carragher insists he won't give up on his title-winning dream until the day he retires.

The Bootle-born defender has won every trophy available bar the Premier League during an outstanding career which so far has spanned 15 years and included 668 club appearances.

At 33, Carragher knows time is not on his side if the one medal he craves is to be added to his collection.

"I won't stop hoping or believing, but I am realistic enough to know that time is running out for me to win it," our No.23 said.

"It's harder to win the title now than it has ever been. Even finishing in the top four is tougher than ever now – as we've found out.

"When I first broke into the Liverpool side in 1996, United were the top side everyone was looking to challenge.

"Arsenal pushed them more than most and then there was ourselves and Leeds making up the top four. And when Roman Abramovich started splashing the cash at Chelsea, that changed the landscape of football completely. That made it even harder for us to win the league because of the amount of money Chelsea spent.

"Now Man City have taken what Chelsea did to another level. And Tottenham have also come into the equation under Harry Redknapp.

"So instead of having three or four clubs capable of challenging it is now five or six."

Last season saw Manchester United overtake Liverpool's tally of 18 titles – but the centre-back claims there is no chance of him becoming 'obsessed' with thwarting our north-west rivals.

"United got No.19 last season and that hurt everybody connected with Liverpool," he said. "But we can't just sit here hoping they don't win another one.

"If we want to stop them being champions then the best way to do it is to finish top ourselves. It's the same with the Champions League. I don't want to be sat here in 10 years' time talking about the fact that United have won more European Cups than us – and the best way to stop that is to qualify for the Champions League and win it again.

"It has been too long for a club like Liverpool not to win the league, but we can't become obsessed with them in the way they used to be about Liverpool when they couldn't win the title.

"What was it for them – 26 years, was it? We'll be doing what we can to make sure we don't break their record! I think during that time, they also got relegated. I don't think that will ever happen to Liverpool – and you can quote me on that.

"And to be honest, I'll have still had a great career. The most important thing isn't Jamie Carragher, it's Liverpool Football Club.

"I think what the manager has been quick to address is the fact that we haven't had the same strength in depth as other top teams. It can't be just about 1 to 11.

"It's a squad game now because of all the matches and the boss has really prepared for that.

"In the past we have perhaps relied on the likes of Stevie (Gerrard) or (Fernando) Torres a bit too much and I think that's something the manager has been looking to address with the signings he's made."

Information correct at date of publication: August 2011

José Enrique

José Enrique is hoping to add his name to the legion of Spanish greats who have graced Anfield over the years.

The likes of Xabi Alonso, Pepe Reina and Fernando Torres all established themselves as world-class players at Anfield, while stars such as Luis Garcia and Alvaro Arbeloa greatly enhanced their reputations in becoming firm favourites amongst Kopites.

"It's amazing that a lot of Spanish players have played here and I am very proud to be the latest one," Enrique said.

"Pepe was already here of course and there are about six or seven players who also speak Spanish so that is great for me.

"I just want to do my best and give 100 per cent for this club to try and help us win something."

A move to Anfield could improve the No.3's chances of becoming a Spanish international, but he has no hesitation when it comes to describing his main ambition for this season.

Enrique added: "It would be fantastic to get into the Spain squad because for every player it's a dream to play for your country, but my first priority is Liverpool and helping us get back into the top four this year."

Meanwhile, Enrique believes Liverpool can make the 2011-12 campaign a memorable one for the fans.

"It was an amazing feeling for me to put the red shirt on for the first time because this is a fantastic club," he said.

"When the manager told me I was starting for the first game of the season I called up my family because they all wanted to watch the game.

"We want to get back into the top four this season and if we could win the Premier League that would be fantastic, but we have to be realistic. A lot of teams have spent a lot of money and for me this league is the most competitive one in the world.

"Seven teams could finish in the top four but we want to be there and we will do everything we can to make that possible."

Enrique has also revealed his delight at playing in front of the Kop for the first time in a red shirt.

"It was an amazing experience to play in front of the Newcastle fans because we had 45,000 people every game and it is the same here at Anfield.

"I remember playing here for Newcastle last season and the Liverpool fans were fantastic.

"It's an amazing feeling when you walk out onto the pitch and the crowd sing 'You'll Never Walk Alone' before kick-off."

"It was an amazing feeling for me to put the red shirt on for the first time"

The Liverpool BIG Quiz ???

answers on pages 60-61

1 Which former treble winner celebrates his birthday on Christmas Day?

2 Who were Liverpool's first opponents of 2010?

3 Who scored Liverpool's last goal of 2009?

4 Who scored Liverpool's last Anfield goal of 2009?

5 Who does the above player now play for?

6 Who scored our first goal of 2010?

7 Who scored our first Barclays Premier League goal in 2010?

8 Against whom did our first Barclays Premier League victory in 2010 come against?

9 Who scored the winner in the first Merseyside derby of 2010?

10 Which was the last team Liverpool beat at Anfield in the Barclays Premier League under Rafa Benitez?

11 Who scored the last Liverpool goal under Rafa?

12 Who was Liverpool's last opponents under Rafa's reign?

13 Who scored Liverpool's first official goal of 2010/11?

14 Against whom did our first Barclays Premier League victory in 2010/11 come against?

15 Who was Kenny Dalglish's first signing as Liverpool manager?

16 During Kenny Dalglish's first period as Manager, who did Liverpool beat in their last league game?

28

17 Who scored twice in the fixture in question 16?

18 Who was the only Liverpool manager to win the FA Cup during the 1990s?

19 Who scored the first goal in the above final?

20 Which team did Gerard Houllier manage after leaving Liverpool?

21 Who did Liverpool beat to win the Screen Sport Super Cup in 1986?

22 What name is Jesus Fernandez commonly known as?

23 Who is Liverpool's youngest ever player?

24 Against whom did our first Barclays Premier League victory in 2010 come against?

25 Who scored the winner in the first Merseyside derby of 2010?

26 Who scored our second goal in the 1977 European Cup final?

27 What number shirt did John Barnes wear for Liverpool?

28 Which defender made his LFC debut at Old Trafford in 1991?

29 Which Dutch goalkeeper played for Liverpool and Everton?

30 Who scored twice for Liverpool against Bolton at Wembley in 1995?

31 Whose free-kick led to Liverpool's winner in the 2001 UEFA Cup final?

32 Which LFC player was fouled that led to the injury time winner against Everton at Goodison Park in the dramatic 3-2 win in 2001?

33 Who did Liverpool beat in their first Barclays Premier League win of 2010-11?

34 Which former Red was known as 'The Stick' by teammates?

35 Which former Red was known as Chico or Bumper by teammates?

36 Which former Red was known as 'The Kaiser'?

37 Which goalkeeper did Kenny Dalglish sign from Wrexham?

38 What is former Liverpool winger Mark Walters middle name?

39 Against which team did Dani Pacheco make his first start under Roy Hodgson?

40 Which three Kop heroes guest in the acclaimed film 15 Minutes that Shook the World?

Jon Flanagan

Jon Flanagan admits he is far from a complete full-back at this stage of his young career – and has targeted two areas in particular he would like to improve.

The 18-year-old wowed supporters at the end of last season with a series of mature displays after being plucked from the reserves.

He knows it won't be easy to maintain a place in the face of stiff competition from both Glen Johnson and Martin Kelly, but the Scouser is determined to do everything possible to get his name on Kenny Dalglish's teamsheet.

"I just want to continue improving," Flanagan said. "There are areas where I need to get better such as going forward and crossing. I need to work on everything.

"With lads like Glen and Martin there is plenty of competition in the squad. That's always good to have. It means if you do get in the team you have to take the chance. Martin is only a few years older than me. He came in last season and did brilliantly. He showed exactly how to grab an opportunity."

Flanagan's pursuit of pitch time could be aided by a versatility which has already seen him operate in three positions for Liverpool.

"My natural position is right-back but I'd play anywhere for the club," he added. "Left-back is okay too and I came on in midfield against Valencia. I don't mind if I have a new role as a holding midfielder now.

"Playing on either side isn't much different. You have the same job to do, you're just on the other flank. Obviously I'm more comfortable on the right because I'm right-footed, but the left side is fine."

Flanagan has gone from U18 hopeful to a recognisable Premier League footballer in the space of four months.

"It's been a change but I just take it in my stride and just carry on with it," he added. "It feels great signing autographs because it's something I used to do when I was little. I used to get Stevie's and Carragher's."

Flanagan also had words of praise for his manager at the Academy, Rodolfo Borrell.

"He's been great – he started me off at U18 level and he's given me a chance, and here I am now, so I'd like to thank him as well," said the teen star.

"They give youngsters a chance at the Academy – it's just dead good down there now."

" I just want to continue improving "

Steve Clarke

Steve Clarke admits he still has managerial ambitions of his own – but claims a three-year contract working alongside Kenny Dalglish at Liverpool was too good to turn down.

Clarke made no secret of wanting to become a manager after leaving West Ham last summer – but that desire is now on hold after signing a long-term deal as first-team coach under Dalglish.

Clarke said: "Circumstances dictate what happens in football. After I left West Ham I thought I would try my hand at management. Nothing came up in that short period – one or two possibilities but nothing concrete developed.

"Then I came here and I've enjoyed it. Working with Kenny I can improve myself as a coach and a person. I can learn a lot from Kenny as a manager, as I've done from previous managers I've worked with.

"My ambition to be a manager will never go away until I do it. But that's something for the future. For now it's to focus on the job at hand.

"It was a great moment to sign the contract. It's always nice when you get rewarded for doing a good job. It's good to settle everything down and have positive things to look forward to in the future.

"Obviously when you come to a place and you're on a short-term contract, you don't quite put down the roots you should because you're never quite sure if you're going to be there long-term. Now I've got a three-year contract I'll be looking to buy a place and settle down in the Liverpool area.

"We have a decent squad here, a lot of good players at the club. They've shown that for us. We've also got young players coming through. That's been a big plus for everyone at the club this season – the young players have come in and stepped forward and done really well.

"Hopefully we can continue with the nucleus we've got, keep adding one or two kids and maybe improve in one or two areas."

Expectations always rise ahead of any new campaign in L4, but while Clarke is

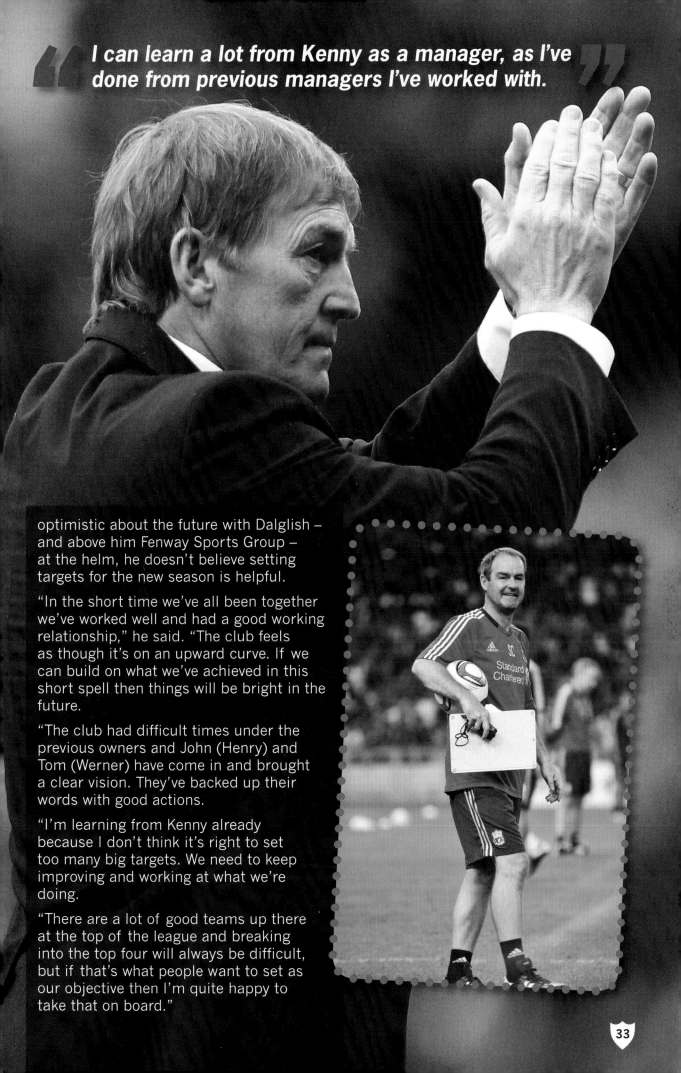

> **I can learn a lot from Kenny as a manager, as I've done from previous managers I've worked with.**

optimistic about the future with Dalglish – and above him Fenway Sports Group – at the helm, he doesn't believe setting targets for the new season is helpful.

"In the short time we've all been together we've worked well and had a good working relationship," he said. "The club feels as though it's on an upward curve. If we can build on what we've achieved in this short spell then things will be bright in the future.

"The club had difficult times under the previous owners and John (Henry) and Tom (Werner) have come in and brought a clear vision. They've backed up their words with good actions.

"I'm learning from Kenny already because I don't think it's right to set too many big targets. We need to keep improving and working at what we're doing.

"There are a lot of good teams up there at the top of the league and breaking into the top four will always be difficult, but if that's what people want to set as our objective then I'm quite happy to take that on board."

Rodolfo Borrell

I always say the same about the fans. Without them Liverpool wouldn't be the club it is.

Rodolfo Borrell has revealed his great pride at following in the footsteps of some of Liverpool's greatest ever names after he was confirmed as the new reserve team coach.

The Spaniard was promoted from his role as U18 coach in an end of season revamp at the club's Academy and admits he was humbled when he learned that some of the Reds' finest managers had cut their teeth in the dugout while with the second-string.

Rodolfo, you've been confirmed as Liverpool's new reserve team coach, congratulations, you must be delighted...

It's a great honour for me to be the reserve team manager. The club have shown they have great confidence in my ability and I am happy. It is a job that means my name will sit forever alongside the likes of Bob Paisley, Joe Fagan, Roy Evans, Phil Thompson and Sammy Lee. They are big names in Liverpool's history and it is also an important role because it is the final step in the Academy. The players need to be ready if they are to make the move into the first-team set-up and I am going to fight for that.

The fans have given the news a big thumbs up, how important is that to you personally?

I always say the same about the fans. Without them Liverpool wouldn't be the club it is. The fans are everything to me and they are very special, backing everyone at the club in good and bad moments. If they have received this news as positive then that is massive for me. I am thankful that they respect me as a person, my ability in my job and especially for the way they have come to Kirkby to watch the U18 games. I will work hard to make them come to more games in the future.

You'll be working even more closely with Frank McParland now - just how important has he been in the Academy's improvement over the past two years?

Frank McParland is my director and we are constantly talking about players, the squad and different situations that arise throughout the season. He is a great support to me and I am certain it will be the same again next season.

What has Kenny Dalglish said to you about your new role and do you expect to have more input from him now?

I cannot complain about the input of Kenny. One of the big things about him is that he hasn't changed since he became first-team manager. He was at the Academy 18 months before he took charge and he still comes to

see us regularly now. It's impossible for him to be here every day like he was when he was based here but he still comes here every week. His input on matters is continual and I go to Melwood more regularly than I used to. We talk about all kinds of things, even the first-team. He sometimes asks my opinion and I will comment. I have to be very thankful to him because without his support it would have been very difficult for me to get the job as reserve team boss. I am very pleased to be working with him and I will make sure I work even harder to help him so that the players can make this last step and be ready for the first team.

You've coached throughout most age groups at youth team level. Do you feel that gives you the perfect grounding to take on your new role?

I have always believed I should coach all of the age groups and go step by step. This has been important as it has helped me to get a big knowledge about the whole process of developing players. At Barcelona I started out with the under eights and moved through all of the age groups. I think I am a lot more ready to make a step forward because of this knowledge and have a very clear idea in my mind about what to do to push the players through to the first-team – or at least get a chance to show what they can do.

Former Reds player Mike Marsh takes over from you as U18 coach - how impressed have you been by him and will you be passing on any advice to him?

He has done a great job with the U16s. Everyone can see he deserves to go through to the U18s. He also has experience playing professionally. I do not need to give him any advice. We talk regularly and I think it is a good move to move him up. He has a great attitude during the training sessions. He has knowledge, experience and I think he will do well.

You had great success at U18 level. Do you expect to take a large part of that group of players up to the reserves with you?

We will have to talk about this. Obviously some players that were U18s are now going to be U19s. We have to discuss whether we will make new signings and who will remain that was already in the reserves' squad. Someone who was U17 could also come through to it. I have only just returned from a tour of the Caribbean and it has only just been confirmed that I am the reserve team manager, so we will talk about all of this in the near future.

Steven Gerrard

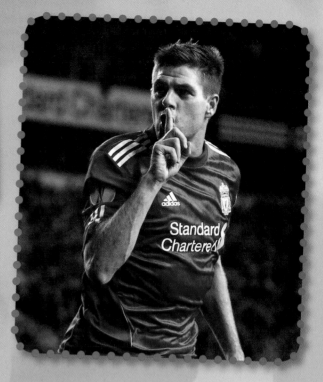

Steven Gerrard says the longest lay-off of his football career has made him desperate to help fire Liverpool to glory this season.

Gerrard underwent surgery on his groin towards the end of last season and missed Liverpool's pre-season tour of Asia as he battled to regain full fitness as soon as possible.

The operation was such a success that the skipper now feels fitter than ever.

"I want to come back with a bang, I want to have a big season," Gerrard said.

"It's been non-stop football for me since I started when I was 17. I've never had a period of more than four or five weeks out of the game, so it's been nice to rest mentally. You don't want to miss games but when you're watching them it gives you that edge, that buzz to get back. I'll come back hungry and hopefully there's a very productive season ahead for me.

"I've had a rest mentally, my injury's coming on well and I can't wait to get going.

"It's important that this team delivers very soon because we've been a number of seasons without putting a trophy in the cabinet and that's not what Liverpool is about. I want to play well, I want to score goals – but it's much more important that the team plays well and we all end the season happy."

Gerrard's determination to 'come back with a bang' means there was no let up in his recuperation this summer, with physios from Melwood working at his holiday home in Portugal every day.

Such professionalism is likely to extend his career for several more seasons but Gerrard is aware that his time wearing Liverpool red – which began at the age of nine – will one day come to an end.

The midfielder's exploits in Istanbul are regarded as his greatest achievement – though the part he played in our 2001 treble and 2006 FA Cup triumph would have been enough to earn most players iconic status.

But our No.8 is not one to dwell on past glories – and instead he is aiming to write at least one more glorious chapter in his extraordinary story before hanging up his boots.

"That's the challenge for me and the players " said Gerrard.

"I want to come back
with a bang, I want
to have a big season."

"We're happy with what we've achieved but there's still a lot of time for me to achieve bigger and better things. I'd like to finish my career with a few more trophies.

"I always look at the 35 marker. If I get there and I'm still involved with Liverpool I'll be delighted but at the moment I'm feeling as good as ever. I've had time to get my body right, get my body strong.

Gerrard's absence from the team has coincided with the emergence of a clutch of Academy products who could become the next generation of Anfield heroes.

Asked how it felt watching the likes of John Flanagan, Martin Kelly and Jack Robinson burst onto the scene just like he did back in 1998, Gerrard replied: "It doesn't feel strange. Other players have done it – Stephen Warnock, Stephen Wright.

"The challenge for those players now is to build on what they did last season – can they become regulars, can they move big players out of their positions."

The 2010-11 campaign will be remembered as a turbulent one in L4, with changes in the dugout and drama in the courtroom dominating the media agenda. Another uncomfortable headline for those with Liverpool in their heart was witnessing Manchester United claim a record 19th league title.

Gerrard added: "As a Liverpool fan and a player it's frustrating when you see your arch-rivals lifting trophies but you've got to give credit where it's due. They've won it, they've overtaken us.

"Now the challenge for us is to equalise. We've got to make sure we've got a squad capable of going into the season and competing with Manchester United."

Joey Barton on Gerrard

"For my generation he's probably as gifted a player as there has been in the Premier League, if not Europe, if not the world.

We're fortunate in this era to have a lot of good players and Stevie is at the top of that tree.

A lot of good players have strengths in one area and weaknesses in other. Stevie has a lot of strengths and very few weaknesses.

He's very, very difficult to play against and that's the reason he's regarded as highly as he is in world football."

Andy Carroll

Andy Carroll has explained why working alongside Luis Suarez at Melwood has given him a genuine belief the pair can provide Liverpool with plenty of goals.

The strike pair, who arrived at Anfield at the start of the year, have already shown signs of a blossoming front-line partnership – and Carroll is convinced the duo's understanding will go from strength to strength as they continue to work alongside each other in training on a daily basis.

He said: "It's been good. In training we've been on the same team and working hard together. We've played games together which has been promising, so I am looking forward to it.

"As you can see, Luis is fast, can get around people and has fast feet, and he has shown he can finish. As we continue to train together, he'll get to know my movements as much as I will know his.

"I'm positive we can score lots of goals for the club."

Carroll's move to Anfield took the footballing world by surprise back in January, but former England striker Alan Shearer believes the ex-Newcastle man will thrive at Anfield.

"Having worked with Kenny, I can tell you he is not only a great man but a great manager. If anyone can get the best out of Andy, then Kenny will," he said.

"Andy has got the chance to work with one of the greatest football figures of the last two decades. I know he will learn the tricks of the trade from Kenny and improve, because I did.

"You can only have respect for Kenny and what he's achieved. I believe Andy's going to a football club with a manager I've got tremendous respect for.

"Kenny will work with him every single day on everything, and develop him massively. He'll pass on tips that he passed on to me when I worked with him, and Andy's going to a great manager who I'm sure will get the very best out of him.

"Andy is a huge loss to Newcastle, and a big gain for Liverpool because there are not many players like him," he said. "He is big, strong, very good in the air and has a good left foot.

"You get that ball in the box and there aren't many that could stop him, so he will be a tremendous asset to Liverpool."

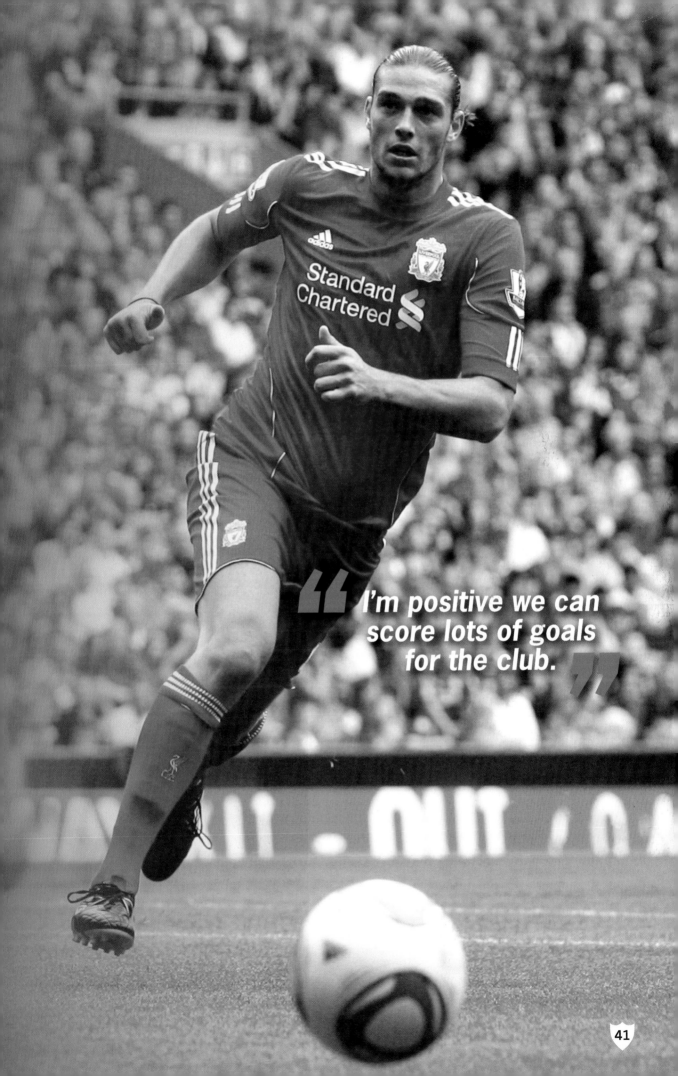

"I'm positive we can score lots of goals for the club."

41

> **Every time I am called upon I know I have to be ready.**

Alexander Doni

Alexander Doni admits he had no hesitation in signing for Liverpool after a strong recommendation from former Kop favourite John Arne Riise.

The Brazilian international played alongside the Norwegian at AS Roma last season and tales of playing in front of the Kop on magical nights at Anfield were never far away from their conversations.

"I spoke a lot about Liverpool with John and he told me what a special club it was," said Doni.

"He spoke about the supporters, the way Liverpool play and this is a very big challenge for me.

"I couldn't turn down the opportunity to come to the Premier League, especially signing for Liverpool which is a huge club in Europe."

With one of Europe's best stoppers guarding Liverpool's goal in Pepe Reina, Doni is certainly under no illusions as to the size of his task at Liverpool in vying for a starting berth.

"Pepe is one of the best goalkeepers in Europe at present and it is an absolute pleasure to work alongside him at this club," he added.

"I will try to help the team as much as I can. Every time I am called upon I know I have to be ready.

"Everybody knows Liverpool already has a fantastic goalkeeper, so any time I am called upon my aim is to do my best.

"I am 31-years-old now so I consider myself to be an experienced goalkeeper. I know I will not be the first choice goalkeeper here to start with but that is not a problem as I knew that before I signed.

"This is a special club to play for and I am enjoying working with Pepe in training. He has been helping me a lot and has already taught me one or two different things.

"I speak some Spanish so I can understand him quite well."

Also helping our new stopper settle in at Anfield are fellow Brazilians Lucas and Fabio Aurelio.

He said: "It's good for me that Liverpool has a few Brazilian players in the team.

One game Doni can't wait to experience is a Merseyside derby having experienced the AS Roma v Lazio Derby della Capitale.

The first meeting of 2011-12 with our rivals across Stanley Park is at Goodison Park on October 1, and it's a date firmly pencilled into Doni's diary.

He added: "The derby in Rome is strongly felt by the supporters because the city just stops for the day and the derby is everyone's main focus.

"From what I've seen on television and from what I've been told the Merseyside derby is very similar, on the pitch at least, so I can't wait for my first experience of this in England."

Luis Saurez

What makes Liverpool different from the other clubs you've played for?

On a human and personal level, if you look inside the dressing room, it takes a special kind of player to play here and you only really discover that when you come to the club and meet everyone in the dressing room. Just as importantly is Kenny Dalglish. I didn't know a lot about him before I came here but I know now I'm playing for a great manager. I knew he was a significant figure in the history of Liverpool but now I know the manager is a very, very important person. He has given me the opportunity to express myself and show what I can do here.

How much did you know about Liverpool when you were growing up?

Of course I remember Liverpool from growing up. They had a lot of great players at the club, particularly forwards. When you are mucking around as a kid you always have a dream of playing at that level and maybe playing for a club like Liverpool. I used to play around pretending to be some of those forwards as a kid.

Did you watch the 2005 Champions League final?

I certainly did, and I'm not the only person who'll remember it for a long time. Aside from the fact it was a great final, Liverpool also really demonstrated they had a spirit and the stomach for a fight. Almost a rebellious attitude in the way they came back. The team was packed full of characters and personalities and they certainly displayed that.

How does it make you feel when the fans sing You'll Never Walk Alone?

It's a great source of motivation for me and the team. It's a well-known song throughout the world of football but when you actually hear it as you're about to go out on the field it's very, very emotional. It gives you a real lift and almost sends a shiver down your spine.

And the fans have a song for you as well – do you know the words?

I can understand the bit where they sing my name! But I'm not sure about the rest of the lyrics. I'm vaguely aware of the song. But the key thing is that when you've been somewhere such a short space of time and the fans give you a song, I suppose it shows you're doing your job quite well.

What are the differences between English and Dutch football?

Football is played in totally different ways in the two countries. Dutch football was an excellent step on the way up to English football for me. If I hadn't gone via Dutch football I think it would have been a difficult step, coming straight into English football. Dutch football allowed me the opportunity to improve my skills, hone myself as a player and improve a few little

details here and there to make sure I was ready to play at the top level. When you come to England it's a lot more intense, the game. It's a higher tempo and you know anything came happen in the 90 or 95 minutes. It's a lot more aggressive and you've got to be ready for anything.

Have you been surprised at how quickly you've adapted?

It's something you always worry about if you move to a different type of football. I was totally aware that everyone was really watching closely. How's he going to adapt to English football? How's he going to settle in? You come here with a reputation and for a lot of money and so people are waiting for things to happen. I've always been of the opinion that if you do the same things you've done throughout your career on the field, if you just concentrate on doing that, then things usually come

right. You have to put aside anything that might be difficult: settling in, the language, getting used to a different culture. Do your job on the field and things will come right.

What makes Kenny Dalglish different from the other managers you've worked for?

The biggest thing is the trust he puts in his players. He trusts us 100 per cent and that makes you want to return that trust and pay it back. We know he's had a long career in football, so we trust in his experience. He's not had that long career for no reason, so we value his expertise.

What do you hope to achieve during your time in Liverpool?

When you play for a club like Liverpool, one of the biggest clubs in England, you've always got to have the aspiration of winning the title. You've got to believe with the quality we've got at this club that this can be a realistic possibility. But we know there is a lot of competition and there are a lot of other teams with the same objective. The next objective is to make sure you're in the Champions League places. We've got to have the confidence that we've got the type of quality here to be aiming for those things. We've got to have an excellent pre-season, prepare really well and then it's a case of being consistent through the season and have a good run of form – not just in flashes through the season.

"I would like to
thank all the fans
who voted for me."

Lucas Leiva

Player of the Year 2010-2011

L.F.C.

Liverpool's Player of the Year for 2010-11 already has his sights set on enjoying another successful season at Anfield this time around.

He may have had to contend with early difficulties in his Liverpool career, but Lucas Leiva now insists he is ready to once again prove himself capable of starring in a successful Anfield side.

The 24-year-old made a total of 47 appearances last year and though he mustered just one goal, it proved to be a spectacular one against Steaua Bucharest in the Europa League.

"I am very happy and really proud to have been picked by the fans," he said, reflecting on his Player of the Year accolade.

"It shows they really appreciate the work I am doing for the team and I will remain the same - always giving 100 per cent in every single game and trying to achieve good things for this club, where I feel really good and want to be a winner.

"I think I am improving every single season, but of course last season was special as an individual for me because I played with consistency. That's what I was looking for in the previous seasons."

He added: "I am really happy with the way I played and I would like to thank my teammates, without them I wouldn't get this kind of award, the staff for helping me every single day on the pitch to improve my abilities, and the fans because to be picked by them is really, really important for me."

The presentation of the award completes a turnaround in fortunes for Lucas, who by his own admission faced initial difficulties in trying to adapt to English football after arriving from Gremio in 2007.

Nonetheless, he believes he emerged a stronger player and person – something he proved on the pitch in 2010-11.

"I wouldn't have expected this (in my first season)," Lucas acknowledged. "The way I started my career at Liverpool wasn't the easiest, but as I have said before, I wouldn't change anything.

"The difficult times just made me stronger and stronger and I tried to improve all the time. That's what I am doing now.

> ## "He has a strong, positive mentality and he deserves all the credit he gets."

"I am looking forward to next season and will try to come back better than I finished this season and try to help Liverpool to achieve good things.

"I would like to thank all the fans who voted for me. I am sure next season we will try to make all the fans happy and that's why we are here – to try and give them success."

Lucas' performances have earned rave reviews off the pitch – while on it his teammates have also spoken of their pride in the way the Brazilian midfielder has gone about his work.

"For me, he's consistently been one of our best players this last season and will hopefully take that into next season," said skipper Steven Gerrard.

Player of the Year 2010-2011

"I've seen first hand the difficulties he's been through. He's basically rolled up his sleeves, worked hard and improved.

"He's got himself stronger in the gym and has never let his head go down, fighting to prove an awful lot of people wrong.

"He has a strong, positive mentality and he deserves all the credit he gets."

England defender Glen Johnson was also fulsome in his praise of the Reds' midfielder.

"There were rumours at the start of the season that Liverpool were going to sell him but the way he's performed just shows you how quickly things can change in football," he said.

"At the minute he's probably one of the first names in the starting 11. He's won the fans over now for sure, so fair play to him. I'm obviously very pleased for him and his family. He deserves the recognition."

Guess Who?

Can you identify the people in
the pictures below?

Answers on page 60

Spot the Difference

Can you see 8 differences between the pictures below?

Answers on page 60

Dirk Kuyt

" we have the quality within the squad to win games "

Dirk Kuyt has insisted Kenny Dalglish's return as Liverpool manager can inspire the Reds to glory this season.

Kuyt admits Dalglish's presence inside the Anfield dressing room has served as a boost to every member of the squad – and he's now looking forward to playing his role in a new-look team this term.

"The most important thing is that he helped us – he helped to give us our confidence back," said the Dutchman. "He convinced us we have a lot of quality, and so far it has been a privilege to work with him.

"He is very popular. The moment he came in, everyone was excited and then when we started to train and work together, everybody started to get even more excited.

"Obviously the results started to come in and everything is looking much better. The mood at Melwood is very good. If you see the lads training, everybody is enjoying it and the games are going very well, so everything is positive.

"I think it is a great move from the owners to give the manager another three years and it will help us move even further forward."

Kuyt is one of several players who embody the change in confidence around Anfield since Dalglish returned to the helm.

"He has done the same with me as he has with all the players," said the 30-year-old. "He gave me confidence. From the first day he arrived, he tried to help me – and that's happened with me scoring goals and providing assists.

"It's also been very helpful bringing some more quality into the team. I am linking up very well with Luis (Suarez), but also in the games Andy (Carroll) has played it has been a privilege to work with him."

Kuyt signed a new long-term Liverpool deal earlier this year and admits it was an easy decision to make once it became clear the positive strides the club were making both on and off the pitch.

"I signed up because I have faith in the club," Kuyt said.

"Everything I noticed shows the ambitions are high. The appointment of Steve Clarke, assistant to Mourinho at Chelsea, is one example. Just a very good on-the-pitch coach. That sort of thing.

"The club strives again to get to a level that suits the club.

"I feel that I am at one of the top clubs in Europe. The goal is still to become champions and win cups, and I will help.

"All we can do is give our best, but we have the quality within the squad to win games and be successful. That's our aim."

Martin Skrtel

> ## "I really think we have a great team and I am lucky to be with these lads."

Martin Skrtel is hoping to build on his 'best ever season' in 2010/11 for Liverpool and help fire the Reds towards glory over the coming months.

The Slovakian defender was one of only two players to play every minute of every Premier League game last season as he established himself as an integral part of the Reds' back-line.

And now he has his sights set on helping Kenny Dalglish's side build on their excellent second half of last year and make a sustained challenge at the top of the table this time around.

"It was probably my best season, because I played every single game," said Skrtel.

"When I came here, a lot of people talked about the way I play, and many said I didn't have the quality to play for Liverpool."

That quality shone through over the course of last season, leaving teammates and fans alike more than confident in their defensive rock.

"It's a fantastic achievement by Martin," said Jamie Carragher. "It's very difficult to play every match the way the modern game is with big squads and rotation.

"There's also the intensity of the games and how many knocks you can get.

"I was hoping that Leighton Baines would maybe get a slight knock in the last game so he would have to come off and Martin could have the record to himself.

"But it's still great for him."

Lucas Leiva, who played in 33 of the Reds' 38 league games last season, added: "Martin has been really good ever since he came to the club and his form has been excellent.

"He is really strong and he gives the midfield confidence that we have a very good centre-back.

"For a defender it's tough to play every game as you can easily pick up yellow cards so his record is very impressive."

So what is the reason behind Skrtel's best form – and how much does he owe to the new manager?

"Rafa Benitez helped me, because he gave me a chance and he also tried to help me every day in training," he explained.

"Sami Hyypia was a great player and also a nice person. He always tried to talk to me and explain things that I could change on the pitch.

"But it wasn't just him. Players like him, Carra, Daniel Agger, Steve, Fernando, Xabi Alonso... I can say every single player from the squad. I could watch them every day in training, and I could learn from them."

He added: "In his first meeting with the team Kenny said to us that we had to trust him and trust ourselves."

"He gave us confidence. He is a great man, a nice person, who tries to talk to us all the time.

"I know he has signed a new contract and I believe he is the right man for Liverpool, a true legend. You could see the results and our improvement on the pitch.

"I really think we have a great team and I am lucky to be with these lads. We didn't fulfil our full potential yet and believe that we can do it very soon.

"But I would like to make our fans happy and proud again so I can promise them that we will do our best this season."

Word Search

Find the words in the grid below. Words can go horizontally, vertically and diagonally.

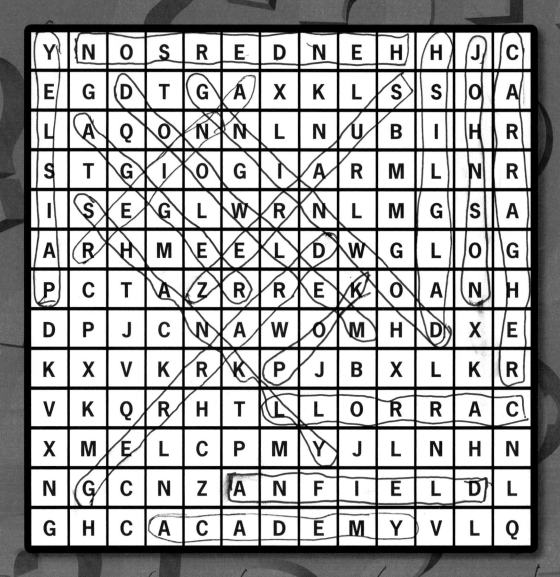

Y	N	O	S	R	E	D	N	E	H	H	J	C
E	G	D	T	G	A	X	K	L	S	S	O	A
L	A	Q	O	N	N	L	N	U	B	I	H	R
S	T	G	I	O	G	I	A	R	M	L	N	R
I	S	E	G	L	W	R	N	L	M	G	S	A
A	R	H	M	E	E	L	D	W	G	L	O	G
P	C	T	A	Z	R	R	E	K	O	A	N	H
D	P	J	C	N	A	W	O	M	H	D	X	E
K	X	V	K	R	K	P	J	B	X	L	K	R
V	K	Q	R	H	T	L	L	O	R	R	A	C
X	M	E	L	C	P	M	Y	J	L	N	H	N
N	G	C	N	Z	A	N	F	I	E	L	D	L
G	H	C	A	C	A	D	E	M	Y	V	L	Q

Academy Agger Anfield Carragher
Carroll Dalglish Downing Gerrard
Henderson Johnson Kop Melwood
Paisley Reina Shankly Suarez

Answers on page 61

Crossword

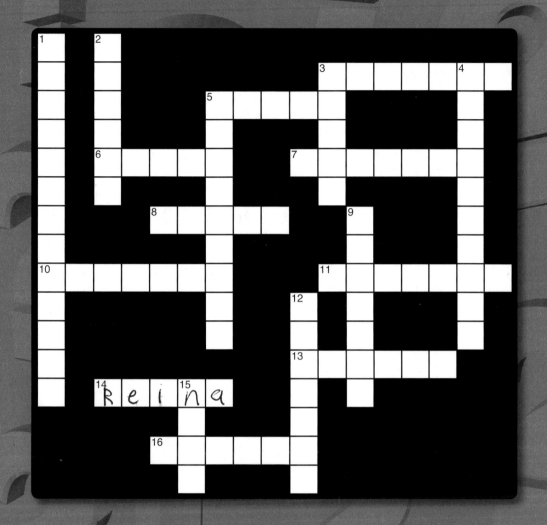

14. R e i n a

ACROSS

3. Manager 1991-1994 (7)

5. Number of First Division Champtionships won by Bill Shankly (5)

6. You'll Never Walk _____ (5)

7. PFA Player of the Year in 2006 (7)

8. Nationality of Dirk Kuyt (5)

10. Charlie Adam previously played for this Glasgow team (7)

11. Country of Luis Suarez's birth (7)

13. This player scored on his 2010 senior debut for Scotland (6)

14. His nickname is Pepe (5)

16. BBC Match of the Day pundit (6)

DOWN

1. Opponents for Liverpool's first-ever Football League match (13)

2. London club defeated 5-2 in penultimate away game of 2010/11 (6)

3. Number of FA Cup wins (5)

4. Liverpool's first league opponents in Season 2011/12 (10)

5. Number of goals Ian Rush scored for Wales (9)

9. Striker signed from Newcastle (7)

12. Winger signed from Aston Villa in July 2011 (7)

15. Player with most European Cup Final appearances (4)

Answers on page 61

Jay Spearing

Jay Spearing has welcomed the added competition for places in Liverpool's midfield, and insisted he is relishing the battle to win a place in Kenny Dalglish's side.

The 22-year-old is determined to build upon an impressive 2010-11 campaign, in which he made 20 first-team appearances and signed a new long-term Anfield contract.

"I've got more competition to fight against now but that doesn't bother me," he said, reflecting on the fact the Reds have signed Charlie Adam and Jordan Henderson during the summer transfer window.

"When you are at a club of this stature you know that in the transfer window they are going to spend money on buying top class players.

"I'm delighted with the signings we've made. Adding Adam and Henderson to the squad is a massive improvement for us. They are both great players.

"From a personal point of view, I wouldn't say them coming in puts extra pressure on me but it makes me fight more.

"I know I need to step up again and prove I can play alongside them or in front of them."

Spearing's extended run in the first team largely coincided with Dalglish's return to the helm in January.

The boss handed the Wirral-born star a regular starting berth as the season drew towards a conclusion, and Spearing is determined to repay the faith show in him.

"Last year was a massive season for me. Roy Hodgson gave me a lot of games and I owe him a lot for that," he added.

"Then as soon as Kenny came in he showed confidence in me straight away by chucking me into the derby.

"Hopefully I repaid that and then he gave me a string of games – nine on the bounce. I just had to keep going and prove that every week I deserved to be out there.

"I've got a lot to thank Kenny for. Hopefully I can now kick on even with the signings who have come in."

Dalglish admits he has been impressed with Spearing's improvement over recent months and is looking forward to the young midfielder progressing further in the future.

"It is great news for us that Jay signed a new deal, great for him and for everybody concerned. It's just reward for the performances he's put in and he thoroughly deserves what he's got.

"He has started games for us, so that is progress in itself as he was never one of the starting XI unless there were injuries or suspensions. But he's in there now and he's in there on merit.

"I think that's progress.

"He's certainly reached a higher level than he has done before. We're delighted with what he's done and he's a great asset for us to have."

Quiz Answers

Page 20 – Spot the Ball

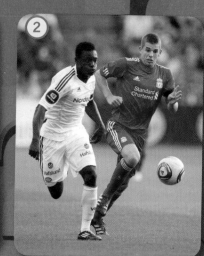

Page 28 – The Liverpool BIG Quiz

1. Gary McAllister.
2. Reading.
3. Fernando Torres.
4. Yossi Benayoun.
5. Chelsea.
6. Steven Gerrard.
7. Sotirios Kyrgiakos.
8. Tottenham Hotspur.
9. Dirk Kuyt.
10. West Ham United.
11. Yossi Benayoun.
12. Hull City.
13. David Ngog.
14. Manchester City.
15. Steve McMahon.
16. Everton.
17. David Speedie.
18. Graeme Souness.
19. Michael Thomas.
20. Lyon.
21. Everton.
22. Suso.
23. Jack Robinson.
24. Tottenham Hotspur.
25. Dirk Kuyt.
26. Tommy Smith.
27. 10.
28. Rob Jones.
29. Sander Westerveld.
30. Steve McManaman.
31. Gary McAllister.
32. Gregory Vignal.
33. West Bromwich Albion.
34. Gary Gillespie.
35. Steve Nicol.
36. Dietmar Hamann.
37. Mike Hooper.
38. Everton.
39. FK Rabotnicki.
40. Steven Gerrard, Jamie Carragher and Dietmar Hamann.

Page 51 – Spot the Difference

Page 50 – Guess Who?

Charlie Adam

Stewart Downing

Andy Caroll

Kenny Dalglish

Page 56 – Word Search

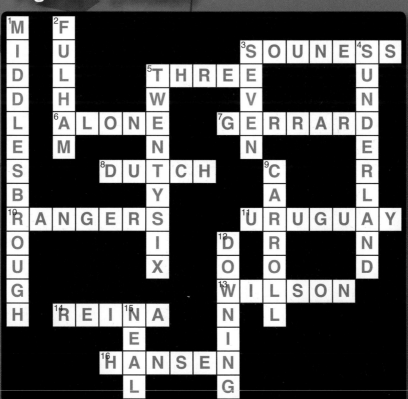

Y	N	O	S	R	E	D	N	E	H	H	J	C
E	G	D	T	G	A	X	K	L	S	S	O	A
L	A	Q	O	N	N	L	N	U	B	I	H	R
S	T	G	I	O	G	I	A	R	M	L	N	R
I	S	E	G	L	W	R	N	L	M	G	S	A
A	R	H	M	E	E	L	D	W	G	L	O	G
P	C	T	A	Z	R	R	E	K	O	A	N	H
D	P	J	C	N	A	W	O	M	H	D	X	E
K	X	V	K	R	K	P	J	B	X	L	K	R
V	K	Q	R	H	T	L	L	O	R	R	A	C
X	M	E	L	C	P	M	Y	J	L	N	H	N
N	G	C	N	Z	A	N	F	I	E	L	D	L
G	H	C	A	C	A	D	E	M	Y	V	L	Q

Page 57 – Crossword

Across:
3. SOUNESS
5. THREE
6. ALONE
7. GERRARD
8. DUTCH
10. RANGERS
11. URUGUAY
13. WILSON
14. REINA
16. HANSEN

Down:
1. MIDDLESBROUGH
2. FULHAM
3. SEVEN
4. SUNDERLAND
5. TWENTYSIX
9. CARROLL
12. DONING
15. NEAL

61

Where's Little Liver?